A Time of Change

by

Valerie Hoadley

Published by New Generation Publishing in 2020

Copyright © Valerie Hoadley 2020

Second Edition

ISBN 978-1-80031-790-1

www.newgeneration-publishing.com

 New Generation Publishing

ABOUT THE AUTHOR

Valerie Hoadley is a retired teacher and lecturer spending most of her working life first in Secondary Schools and then in a Further Education College. She was born in the Lake District and after a period running her family business in partnership with her husband, the couple returned to their chosen profession, teaching, and moved to Norfolk where they spent the rest of their working life. On retirement they went to live in Spain, a country she came to love, describing her time there as "living in Paradise". However, in 2007 they returned to England and, looking forward to a new phase in their lives, settled in an area unknown to them, Launceston, Cornwall. It was not to be. Within 6 months, out of the blue, her husband was diagnosed with cancer and less than a month later he was dead. Suddenly, without children, she found herself alone in an area she had scarcely begun to know, her few relatives and many good friends far away. As she fought to deal with her loss and make a new life she began to write down her experiences. A good friend happened to see this and urged her to publish, saying it could help others. She had not thought of such a thing but knew then that if it could help even one other person going through such a terrible time then she must do it. The first edition of this book was the result. Many have contacted her to say the book helped them to cope with their own losses of a loved one and her hope is that this second edition may help many more, for Coronavirus has indeed caused "a sea change" in peoples lives. The grim numbers of deaths are published every day, but what of the even larger numbers of the bereaved around the world; those who have lost a beloved spouse, a mother or father, sister or brother, aunts, uncles, nieces, nephews, cousins, dear friends and more? These are the ones who are having to cope with the terrible grief and desolation that death can bring, and fight to overcome it.

Where this book quoted from work which may still be under copyright, every effort has been made to contact the copyright holders and in all cases the source has been acknowledged.

The Author wishes to thank all those who have responded to her request, and in every case have given permission.

The quotation from Mary Rogers is taken from her book "How to be a Merry Widow, Life after Death for the Older Lady" published by Third Age Press Ltd.

Preface

We met at 19 and married at 23 and so for more than half a century he was the centre of my life. No he was more than that, he was my life for we joined our lives, our time, our work and our interests, our thoughts, ideas and philosophies, not that we were identical, for our partnership was all the stronger for the individuality, the strengths and the weaknesses we each brought to it, but we were two atoms of different elements that joined to make a single new entity and in that we were at home.

We spent our working lives in Britain and when we retired went to live in Spain. Our time there was like time spent in paradise but after 15 years we set off again and settled in Cornwall for a new stage of our lives. However it was not to be, for within a few short months, without warning, we were suddenly and brutally torn apart.

A lifetime spent together that now seems oh so short. The surviving element can never form that entity again. He was gone never to return. He lives now only in my memory and the memories of those who knew and loved him. Yes I carry him with me, and that is all I have left to ease the pain of my loss. It not enough but it is all I have left.

A TRIBUTE TO MY HUSBAND BRIAN L.HOADLEY

Every loss of a loved one is different depending on so many factors but although mine was a single unique and very private experience, just as a raindrop falling into the sea becomes indistinguishable from it and one with it, so my drop of pain is also a small part of the ocean of a universal human experience of loss.

I hope therefore that this work might be a sharing, and a sharing that might even be a small consolation or comfort to those who have to tread the same stony path. If it could be such to even one person I would be content.

No man is an island
Entire of itself.
Every man is a piece of the continent.
A part of the main.

Each man's death diminishes me,
For I am involved in mankind,
Therefore never send to know
For whom the bell tolls
It tolls for thee.

John Donne 1573 – 1631

"A lovely, broad, foaming highway stretching all the way back
to the Spain I love"

A TIME OF CHANGE

One woman's journey through a sea change of life

May

I watched as the ship slipped away from the quayside and
held out my hand but already Spain was beyond my grasp.
The gap between me and the land of Spain that had been my
home for more than 15 years slowly widened until the
quayside became the bay, the bay became coastline and the
coastline became the open sea. Part of me still couldn't
believe it. It had been his tentative suggestion that perhaps it
might be the best thing for us to return to England and
perhaps we should at least think about it. It had come as a
surprise as I had always said that I would never leave our
lovely Spanish villa and although from that moment on we
had thought it through and agreed together that it was our
best option, it still seemed so strange that we should be doing
this. The rain had started before we turned away from the

sight of the Mediterranean Sea and continued all the way as we drove right across Spain to the north coast and the Bay of Biscay. It was as if the angels were weeping to see us leave. The breeze freshened as we gathered speed across the open sea but I stood at the rail and watched the ship's wake make a lovely, broad, foaming highway stretching all the way back to the Spain I loved and the life we had shared there so happily now all over and gone.

The rain had finally stopped but all was grey – the sea and the sky and that highway stretching back to all that was now over. Come, he said "it's getting cold, its time for a drink and its time to look forward to a new phase in our life."

As we sat in the warmth of the ship and looked out at the ever changing sea my spirits lifted and I enjoyed the moment. We walked again on the deck and the restless waters, the fresh sea breezes, the leaping dolphins and eventually the thin smudge of the coastline on the horizon all spoke to us of movement, change, and a new life. I looked back once more and whispered to Spain a good bye and a promise to return many times and then I turned to the smudge that had become a firm dark line. As it grew bigger and unfolded its curves and heights so my spirit embraced it and a shiver of excitement at all that was to come encompassed me. I thought of that coast with its lovely bays and headlands, its pretty villages and exhilarating cliff top walks. I thought of the full flowing rivers, the wooded valleys, the rolling fields and country towns, I thought of the brooding landscapes of the windswept moors, the jagged tors and the remnants of peoples long gone. I thought of the roadside banks and hedgerows embroidered with wild flowers, of the homely cows and sheep in the fields, the horses on the country lanes. I thought of the sunlight dancing on water, the rain drenched hills, the eerie light of an approaching storm over the open moors, the moonlight silvering the peaceful landscapes. In short I thought of the rich tapestry that is Cornwall and all it has to offer, so much to explore together, to see and to do. A new phase indeed, exciting and beautiful.

We have arrived and the new house beckons, eager to be at last turned into a home. Slowly over those first days and weeks chaos evolves into order as a new place is found for each piece of our former lives. The little cupboard, the first piece of furniture we ever bought, now fifty years old. It has served us well – first in its original intended capacity as a record cabinet but over the years used for gardening sundries and notes, for drinks, and for music tapes, adapting as we changed. I look at it, still handsome in its lovely wood but now filled with memories, oh yes a place must be found. And so it is with every piece uncovered, large or small they are part of our life. Some like the little cabinet have travelled with us all the way along life's path; others are newer and mark stages and stops along the way – English books, Dutch figures, Spanish furniture, and French porcelain.

Then there are the people – those who are in and are part of our home through their gifts – gifts from France, Holland, South Africa and Spain; from family past and present; gifts from schooldays, 21st birthdays and wedding gifts from those who knew us in our youth; gifts from colleagues and friends during our working lives; and later from our retirement years each holding a memory of a relationship, and treasured because of it. Finally our own memories, photographs, souvenirs and gifts shared and exchanged and so the house becomes our home. Yes we can be happy here.

We take a break with a very good friend to celebrate a birthday and our new life in Cornwall. A magical day of rest, relaxation, love and friendship in elegant surroundings with beautiful views, fine wine and exquisite food, and in the background the peaceful sea we so recently crossed.

We do not know.

August

For our anniversary we go to Plymouth and stay overnight to take in a show. We enjoy a celebration meal, drink in the sights, and dissect the performance we had seen, as is our way. The trip is a great success and I thought perhaps the start of a new tradition, for …..

We do not know.

Summer & Autumn

The summer passes so swiftly, so busily. We start to explore, just a small beginning for we have as yet had so little time but hope to have so much more. First Launceston our new home, such an attractive little town, so steeped in history and surrounded by beautiful countryside, no wonder we both fell in love with it as soon as we saw it; then the south coast – Mevagissey and Gorran Haven; the north coast – Tintagel and Boscastle, the interior Bodmin Moor, Roadford Lake and Lanhydrock. We shared golden days of adventure and contentment. There is so much more to explore together, to see and to do.

We do not know.

October

A card for my wife

To some, romance means candlelight, wine and roses, gifts are special, but they fade with time.

To me, romance is simply being with you,
Sharing each special moment together, day after day.

I know in my heart that you'll always be here for me,
And that's the best gift you could ever give me.

You're wonderful in every way, and that's why I'll
Always be here for you, too. You mean everything to me.

I love you and I'm wishing you all the happiness in the
World on your birthday.

With all my love today, tomorrow and always.

We do not know.

November

Christmas approaches and plans are made, cards are
bought, gifts are chosen, recipes are checked. A small
problem arises, nothing serious just a few tests.

We still do not know.

December 17th

I cross my bridges when I come to them and not before.
Today brought not just a bridge but a thunderbolt from the
blue. The brief tests are over and give confirmation. " I'm
very sorry there is nothing I can do" the surgeon said. We
sat stunned in silence unable to speak or move. At length
the doctor broke the silence "Does this come as a shock to
you?" I looked across to him. "Well yes it does, I have felt
so well. All summer I have felt so well". We drove home
in silence. We wept.

We did not know but now we do.

I go shopping. Its Christmas time and the aisles are thronged with shoppers. Children, happy and impatient, shout and play – but I do not hear them. The music blares but it can't reach me. The displays are tempting – but not to me. Mothers push laden trolleys and their excited young ones race around. I race too for I must get back to him. I look at the goods but they blur before my eyes and I need all my strength to stop the tears from falling. I look at the people but they seem a million miles away. It's as if am walking in a bubble, I can see out of it but it imprisons me. People speak to me but they are beyond the barrier. They can't reach me and I can't reach them.

I am in a different world.

January

Less than a month later it is all over. The unbelievable happens, its course so swift and unstoppable. Every day I thought "it can't get worse" but every day it did. We went on through the deteriorations, the weakness and the suffering; the struggles, the falls and the crises, and through it all his humour and bravery shone out. Then came the evening when I had to tell him "the doctor says that if you refuse to go into hospital you could die during the night". Refuse he did, as I knew he would. "I'll take my chance" he said.

Whatever happens we will be together until the end – "until death do us part". He did not die and we struggled on. I looked at the familiar face now so unfamiliar like an El Greco painting. I looked at the wasted limbs so recently so strong. We were helped, supported and nursed with such kindness and efficiency. I got through the days and the nights in shock. I took charge, made decisions, cared for him and protected him and the memories are a jumble of concern and despair – my fear, his bravery, their kindness, sympathy and love. Lower we sank, senses dimmed: morphine was his final aid and mine was the concern and love of those – friends and professionals alike – around me in person or with me by phone and email, holding out to me their love and their skills to carry me through the unbelievable.

Death came peacefully and quietly in the stillness of the early hours. It was over. Cancer had swiftly and silently done its worst. He was gone never to return. At least I had to be grateful that he was out of his suffering and as yet I was unaware of the true nature of mine. Grief came like a tornado.

Our life was over.   My existence remained.

"It is with the deepest sorrow that I tell you ….."

"It is with the deepest sorrow that I tell you ….."

And ever has it been that love knows not its own depth until the hour of separation.

Kahlil Gibran 1883 - 1931

To my Dear and Loving Husband

If ever two were one then surely we,
If ever man were loved by wife then thee,
If ever wife were happy in a man,
Compare with me ye women if you can,
I prize thy love more than whole mines of gold,
Or all the riches that the east doth hold,
My love is such that rivers cannot quench,
Nor ought but love from thee give recompense,
Thy love is such I can no way repay,
The heavens reward thee manifold I pray

Anne Bradstreet 1612 – 1672

There is this woman

She goes about her daily tasks,
Takes charge, she talks she even smiles,
She takes decisions, she makes her choices.

Who is this woman so in control?

She is not I for I am here,
Torn and bleeding on the floor,
Prostrate with grief and desolation.
She is not I for I am here

To the world you may be just one person
But to one person you may be the world

Anon

A Service

The day has dawned and all is ready. Friends are gathered, support is on all sides. Follow roses of England, carnations of Spain; follow that last journey for a service must begin

"We have come to the lovely Glynn Valley to honour the life"
"A time of reflection and meditation"
"It is natural we should be sad today"
"The loving and devoted husband who was friend, companion, guide and soul mate all in one"
"Respected colleague"
"Friend, educator, spokesman"
"Champion of many in difficulties"
"Reflect on life in Spain – a time shared with many friends"
"Remember him with happiness and love"
"Human life is built on caring"
"We remember….. We are grateful to have known and loved him"
Jesus said:

"Peace I leave with you; my peace I give to you"

Our Father Who art in Heaven
Hallowed be thy name; thy kingdom come
Thy will be done on earth as it is in heaven
Give us this day our daily bread
And forgive us our trespasses
As we forgive them that trespass against us
And lead us not into temptation
But deliver us from evil.
Amen

Debussy, Bach and Beethoven,
Loss, Desolation and Pain

"We say our final goodbyes"
"Contemplating our unity with the earth and all forms of
life and existence".

**Life and death are one, even as the river and the sea
are one ....
For what is it to die, but to stand naked in the wind and
to melt into the sun
And what is it to cease breathing but to free the breath
from its restless tides
So that it may rise and expand and seek your God
unencumbered**

Kahlil Gibran

Celtic benediction

May the road rise to meet you
May the wind be always at your back
May the sun shine warm upon your face
The rain fall soft upon your fields
And until we meet again may your God hold you in the
hollow of his hand

Share your thoughts and feelings on his life, talk about him
often, repeat the words and sayings he used and enjoy your
memories of him just as you have today, resolving that you
who live on, will use your lives more fully and to better
purpose for having known him or for having shared in his
life.

-Our Love-

A fleeting smile, an upward glance
A gossamer silken web
A snowflake pure, a blossom rare
A hint of perfume on the air
A sparkling dewdrop on a petal
The rainbow of the soul
                              The fragility of our love
The trusting arms of a tiny child
An outstretched hand to clasp in mine
The melting of the winter snows
The welcome breath of spring
The shimmering of the noon heat haze
The flickering of the fireside flame
                              The warmth of our love
The fire of a diamond or sunlight on water
The sheen of a pearl or moonlight at night
The grace of a ballet or leaping gazelle
The magic of dawn, the glory of sunset
The velvet bloom on a dusky rose
Beyond all these
                              The beauty of our love
The fortress on the rocky keep
Protecting those within
A shelter from the storms of life
The winds that blow, the heated air
A granite bluff in the quick sands of time
Steady, unfailing and true
                              The strength of our love
This golden ring around my finger
Encirclement without a join
A unity unasked, unbidden
Two hearts in one, at one, at home
A seamless robe, a trinity
A fore hint of heaven
                              The truth of our love

February

Dust to dust – Ashes to ashes

FAREWELL

You had to leave me and it broke both our hearts
Now you have gone and I can't trust myself to speak
So another must say these last words of farewell
But no matter, for words are beyond us two now

Here you must rest while I go on alone
To face a future I must make for myself
Though sad and empty I must make myself live
And do my best with the time I have left

But though I feel lonely I'm not really alone
You live in my memory and heart so forlorn
There you will stay and be with me still
In good times and bad, just as before

So we'll journey together until the day comes
When I may return here and lie on this hill
Come here to join you in death as in life
Just part of creation, a man and his wife

March

To a friend

You are a pearl in the centre of my existence
Like a jewel in a ring
You are a soft and gentle lustre
Gleaming in the light of my life

You stayed and helped and supported

In your kind and thoughtful way
And when dark death descended
Bore me up in your loving embrace

Your gentleness calmed my spirit
Your sympathy eased my pain
In good times and bad you're a treasure
And truly a pearl beyond price

To have even one good friend is to keep the darkness at bay

Pam Brown 1948 –

A faithful friend is a strong defence – he that hath found one hath found a treasure

The Bible – Sirach 6

Friendship is a candle whose flame grows brighter when the hour is darker

Anon

Friendship is a sheltering tree

Samuel Taylor Coleridge

Meeting Old Age

For so long, half a century, life flowed broad and mighty
as a river. Swift moving, ever changing, yet flowing in a
fluid continuity;
Ever onwards past rolling hills under weeping skies of
grey clouds. Onwards through broad sunlit meadows under
the great blue beyond
Now tossed by rapids or dancing through rocks
Now meandering slowing or stilled by deep pools
Surged by the wind, calm under the stars.
We swam through it all – the obstacles and the blessings,
Content and together in both the struggles and the ease.

Then the thunderbolt struck and with so little warning –
Everything gone; just the empty blackness, the icy void,
the disbelief
It struck us down, prostrate and helpless.

I stir into consciousness, hot tears, cold despair, moaning
grief, disbelief,
In a trance I fashion a dream, take charge, plan, write,
decide, but it's not real
Friends, support, sympathy and praise; flowers, a journey,
a leaving, but it's not real.
And always in me and with me, around me and on me,
Touching others too and reflecting back,
Is that immense total blackness, a night of the soul,
Like the void of space itself, the silent empty void between
the worlds.

Then its over, all are gone. All is gone –
The dream bubble bursts and I face a closed door.
There is nowhere else to go and I know I have to open it
and step inside.
I do so and enter a strange land.

I know no one around me but in the distance I see known and loved faces.

At my feet is a pool, dark, still and deep. I look down and see a reflection. It is of an old woman grey and lined, her head is bowed with the weight of the years, her sad eyes reflect the experience of age.

I turn, but no one is there. The reflection is my own; catapulted by the thunderbolt into a new existence, hurled into old age by its mighty blast.

I bow to what must be and start walking on – one step after another.

Life is no longer a river but a stony path into the future and I have no choice but to follow it, alone.

A Widow's Hymn

How near me came the hand of Death,
When at my side he struck my dear,
And took away the precious breath
Which quicken'd my beloved peer!
How helpless I am thereby made!
By day how grieved, by night how sad!
And now my life's delight has gone,
Alas! How am I left alone!

The voice which I did more esteem
Than music in her sweetest key,
Those eyes which unto me did seem
More comfortable than the day;
Those now by me, as they have been,
Shall never more be heard or seen;
But what I once enjoyed in them
Shall seem hereafter as a dream.

Lord! Keep me faithful to the trust
Which my dear spouse reposed to me:
To him now dead preserve me just
In all that should performed be!
For though our being man and wife
Extendeth only to this life,
Yet neither life nor death should end
The being of a faithful friend.

George Wither 1588 – 1667

April

The Lie

Every day I live a lie, I know but I can't help it.
I've made new friends, I do new things,
I'm out and about and I'm busy.
I reassure my long time friends.
Respond to kindness with a smile.
I've got my music and my books.
And then there is the garden.

But its all an act, it's just not real, I really do not want it.
I have filled my life, as I know I must.
And recognise that is good.
But whatever I do and wherever I go
And however normal I seem
The eggshell can break, at a word or a sound –
For all I want is what I have lost.

A few friends see beyond the act and what would I do
without them.
They bear me up, they keep me going
My only links with what was and what is
Then the silent witnesses of my grief

My constant feline companions;
They sense that things are not the same
They smell the lie and huddle close.

I do not want to live a lie it goes against the grain
But if I want to live at all it seems the only option
"Time," so they say, "will have its effect,
Don't be so hard on yourself
You will learn to merge the old with the new,
Remember with fondness, move on with hope
And no longer live a lie"

But still I go on and nothing changes, still living the lie,
The interests are there and I can respond
But I cannot hold on for long.
For my reality is cold and dark
And its shadow blots out the sun.
For all I want is what I've lost
And all the rest is a lie

Sometimes I'm there

Sometimes I'm there in that strange new world and I think
of my friends and smile:
I think of my cats, I think of my home and I think of my
garden and smile.
I look at his picture, remember his sayings, think what we
did and I smile.
Perhaps for an hour or nearly a day acceptance enters my
soul
But then like a mirage it fades and dissolves and I reach
out to grasp it in vain:
For I'm back in the darkness falling to limbo surrounded
by chaos and pain.

May

Guilt

The longed for ease has slipped into my soul
And a calm has settled over my being.
For three days now, the keel of my ship
Has responded to my touch;
My vessel has been even, its course has been steady.
Such blessed relief to my weary spirit.

In my sudden awareness of its stealthy approach
My mind looks back and sees its progress.
A new sensation courses through me
And I feel guilty. Guilty? Yes, Guilty!
How can I engage with life in this way
While he is gone to a cold dark grave!
I am angry, oh so angry with myself,
"What is the matter with you?" Are you mad?"
You have tried so hard these last long months
To pick yourself up off the floor.
Crushed and broken but knowing you must rise
Trying to rise and falling once more
Torn and bleeding back to the floor.

Now at last the first stirrings of success
Three days of relative calm, Are you relieved,
Are you grateful or proud of yourself?
You have tried so hard
You have struggled so long
And now you feel guilty – Are you mad?

No, not mad, I know I must go on
I know I must walk in the life-giving sun
But my heart's in the grave, my spirit at his side
And every fibre in my being screams out
For I shudder to walk away from him
And I don't want to carry on.

So this first success,
welcome though it is,
is also a new kind of pain.
It lets me know I have taken at last
Those first few faltering steps away
So unwelcome, resisted and foreign.

I never walked away before
Not once in fifty years
So yes I feel guilty and yes I feel pain
To engage with life when he cannot
I want so much to take him with me
How can I smile at the life-giving sun?

Catherine Wordsworth

**Surprised by joy-impatient as the wind –
I turn'd to share the transport – O with whom
But Thee – deep buried in the silent tomb,
That spot which no vicissitude can find**

**Love, faithful love recall'd thee to my mind –
But how could I forget thee Through what power
Even for the least division of an hour
Have I been so beguiled as to be blind**

**To my grievous loss. That thought's return
Was the worst pang that sorrow ever bore
Save one, once only when I stood forlorn,
Knowing my heart's best treasure was no more,
That neither recent time nor years unborn
Could to my sight thy heavenly face restore.**

William Wordsworth 1770 - 1850

A Birthday Revisited

Last year was remembered, revisited:
The pleasure and contentment, the innocence of not
knowing, the hidden support of the unforeseen, the kindness
of that veil. I remembered his warmth, his humour and his
hope.

Friends old and new were with me:

The gracious surroundings so English and unchanging, the
enduring bays and headlands, the eternal restless sea, all
were still there, but of course he was not.

The solitary visit came later;
The valley lay so peaceful in the gentle encircling hills, it
was hard to believe in that silent scene, as I stood so calm
on that tranquil green, the torrential anguish of loss within.

June

He is not here

I wake; and I remember
He is not here.
The sun rises, the birds still sing.
Everything seems the same
But he is not here.

The rugs he made are still on the floor
But he is not here.
His pictures hang upon the wall
His photographs look at me
But he is not here.

Some days I can't believe it
He is not here?
His friends are here, life goes on
Everything seems the same
But he is not here

Other times it's all too clear
He really is not here.
Its everything else that seems unreal
Swims around me like a mirage
but he really is not here.

And then I know the awful truth
Because he is not here
Things seem the same but they're not the same
And for me they never will be again.
Because he is not here.

We must not allow the clock and the calendar to blind us to the fact that each moment of life is a miracle and mystery.

**Attributed to H.G. Wells 1866 – 1946
But the source has not been verified.**

If only he could know

If only he could know, know how life has been for me
Know of these months of tears and pain, grief and desolation
Know of the void he left in my heart that nothing else can fill
Really know how hard it's been, to walk away alone.

It's not that I want him to feel my pain or wipe away my tears

But if he could know, just for a moment, then he would understand
The true extent of my love for him and the place he holds in my heart
Really know how strong it is even now I'm alone.

We think we know the depth of our love as we tread life's path together
But in the turmoil of life our hearts are veiled even from ourselves;
We take for granted our continued existence, our sharing, support and love
Until a life stops……..and then………
……….we see that the words of the poet are true

And ever has it been that love knows not its own depth until the hour of separation

Kahlil Gibran

July

A Return

How good to feel again the warm soft air
And gaze once more over the shimmering sea,
With a welcome as warm as the southern sun
From friends so dear to me.

I feared to make this trip alone
And without him stand on the soil of Spain,
But I look at the faces of the two I meet
And I feel so at home again.

So good to feel part of the exuberant life

Of the Spain I have come to love so well;
The colours, the flowers, the food, the wine
Even the wanderers with goods to sell.

We share precious hours of beauty and warmth
We walk and talk and reminisce;
We fill our time with so many good things
We discuss and plan and promise.

So few short days but in that time
I begin to learn to live again;
To look back with fondness and forward with remembrance
To accept their understanding which lessens the pain.

Too soon it is over and I must go
The parting has turned my heart to stone
Desolation returns, my vision blurs
I have never felt so alone.

Friendship, a dear balm.......
A smile among dark frowns: a beloved light:
A solitude, a refuge, a delight

Percy Bysshe Shelley 1792 – 1822

August

A Wedding Anniversary

The day began calm and grey, faithfully reflecting my mood, facing it alone I had feared its arrival so planned its hours with care.

The early visit to the spot where he lay was filled with a desolate peace but while I was there the sun came out as if to smile at me.

My steps were drawn to the tranquillity of Lanhydrock where so recently we'd shared such content.

I strolled through the gardens where we have strolled, I had thought that I couldn't do it but the beauty and form of the plants in the sunlight, the colours and sounds of life brought to my soul an acceptance and stillness and I almost enjoyed my time there.

I retraced our steps to seek refreshment, just as I had planned to do and thought how different was this day, from the anniversaries we'd shared together, but even if only for this one special day, I was able to think back with love; remember the good times, keep pain at bay and hold him close to my heart.

Later, alone, I walked through the parkland that had been his especial joy, the enduring trees, the encircling hills, protective and lovely still. The beauty of the scene was almost unbearable since he was not here to see it but I carried on and followed my plan and it supported and kept me going.

I thought of last year, how different it was in the bustle of the busy city, we went to a restaurant, we went to the theatre, we shopped and gazed and talked. We thought it was the first of many such trips now we were settled in Cornwall. We even made plans, thought we'd start a tradition, one we'd follow in years to come.

Then I drove through the countryside exploring new sights that I planned to share with others. Railways and castles, green fields and pastures, to become part of the future. A future I did not want to embrace, though I knew I had to do it. So I followed my plan and made a few more before the day was over.

Later as I returned to familiar roads, I felt quite proud of myself; I had followed my plan, achieved my goals, even enjoyed a few moments. Retribution would come, I knew that it would, I had only staved off the moment; desolation would return, grief would overcome but I had lived through this day and survived.

The Rain in Cornwall

My tears fall like rain in immeasurable drops I know not when they come, nor when they will go but they are a constant feature of the climate of my life. The rain of grief in all its phases is like the rain of the heavens in all its forms. At first it is expected in the shock and finality of Death like the downpour presaged by the gathering storm clouds. As the darkness, the sultry heat and the cold sharp stinging drops so the soul's darkness, the hot tears, and the cold desolate painful loss.

I stand on the moor in a pool of sunlight and gaze over the brooding landscape at the distant dark clouds. The scene has a majestic beauty; the rolling moors, the jagged Tors, the lowering, ominous clouds bending to touch the waiting earth. The golden light gilds every blade of grass and the very air glistens with its beauty.

Though awed by its stark magnificence I am afraid. I have seen this before, and know what is coming. Like the earth I wait and soon the pattering begins, becomes a fall and then a blast that soddens the yielding soil. Nor is there any escape for me as dark thoughts cause the first gentle tears to roll and quickly become a torrent of grief. I must be strong and turn my thoughts to new and positive things.

The time I have left must be given purpose for something good must come out of this pain. And so I am busy with this and that, I join and smile and act. But it isn't just storm clouds that cause the rain. The passing squall, or April shower can come from the innocent sky.
So what is this from out of nowhere?

Someone was kind to me; I heard a tune or saw a gesture; I remembered a place, a phrase, a smile, a garden or a flower.

Any of these is enough to cause the rain to fall. Strangest of all – "nothing" can cause the rain to fall even on the pleasantest of days.

To me the meanest flower that blows can give thoughts that do often lie too deep for tears.

William Wordsworth

September

The way is hard

I look in the mirror and scarcely recognise what I see, that face so lined with pain, so greyed by grief, so changed in so few months, it can't be me?   I do not care, it is nothing to me, and I'm totally indifferent. It could be a stranger standing there, in a way I suppose it is. When death strikes one down and takes that one he strikes others too and leaves his mark behind.

Then a stab of fear pieces my heart, beware, take heed, it whispers. Look and take heed, understand what you see, you have to fight back, you have to be strong. If you don't beat this, then it will beat you and the rest of your time will be wasted. You don't want that and neither would he, he relied upon you to be strong.

I don't know if I can heed that warning, I only know I must try but the landscape's so bleak and the way so hard that I falter and stumble and fall. So many times as I struggle on, the sun comes out from the clouds I reach for the moment and live in its light, but then it is gone, the moment is past and the darkness claims me again.

If you cry because the sun has gone out of your life, your tears will stop you from seeing the stars

Rabindranath Tagore 1861 – 1941

Dewdrops

I see a dewdrop on a rose, its beauty sparkles in the sun it gives me hope, it makes me smile and shows me what to do. The support of a friend, an experience shared, the beauty of nature,a kindly act, I must gather these dewdrops to water my soul and perhaps some day in the light of the sun they'll bring life to my spirit once more.

Crossing a line

A seedling has pushed into my soul, so tiny and fragile its barely there but this speck of life, of something new struggles to survive and makes its mark. Yesterday it wasn't there but now there is this change.

What is this new born in my heart? A feeling that wasn't there before. It's almost peace but not quite yet. Well acceptance then or resignation? Has time at last pitied me and led me into the present?

I've dwelt in a land of my own these months, not in the present nor in the past. The past is gone and I can't be there where each fibre of my being yearns to be and I'm not in the present, though I've tried so hard, for those steps lead away from him.

This feeling is fickle I know it won't stay. Some days will be hard and I'll slip back again, but nevertheless a change has occurred. Though the seedling's too weak to make a great change I can nurture that seedling let in the sun, and help it grow to the light.

And now this tiny speck of life reaches up and touches me. The mists of my foreign world recede and the past slips away from my clinging grasp. I bow my head in pain and grief but the present embraces me.

I do not want this though I've striven so hard to reach this place where I now seem to be. Success in survival is failure to stay. After all these months I accept the present, face the break, acknowledge reality. No longer live the lie.

Time may have reached out its hand to me may have planted the seed and pulled me on but its not stemmed the bleeding nor lessened the shock, not dulled the pain nor blunted the grief but nevertheless something is different something is calmer within.

Its not a betrayal it's what he would want. He'd tell me to cling to the present and live. To go with the friends who've supported me well, reach out to the new ones and share in their interests. Carry him with me ever in my heart, remember with love and acceptance.

October

And so I moved on and into a new reality. Another month begins and the new feeling is still with me. October starts with another birthday, this time my own – the first in fifty three years that he has not shared, except in memory. However I had planned this day and although this time I feel HIS loss – that he can't be here, that now he will never reach this age – more keenly than I feel my own, it follows its course without collapse, buoyed up as I am by family and friends rallying round, contacting, supporting and spoiling me.

Reaction came later, as I knew it would, as it always does, but despite the bad times the new feeling, now weakened, now stronger, remained. However tentatively, I am back in the present, and however painful it is, I acknowledge that he is in the past.

It is a new strength and, oh dear…….a new pain.

November

Death is a part of life

Is it the season that has caused this relapse, for death is all around me?

The season is mellow and filled with great beauty though the autumn days grow shorter, the flowers of summer continue to bloom but are joined by the tints of the fall, the seeds and the berries, the nuts and the fruits shine out of their russets and golds, and then come the leaves in their moment of glory, lighting their trees like a torch; catching the light in the pale autumn sun, the spectacle catches our breath but in the morning mist their beauty is muted and we feel the shudder of death for we know that their hues are the colours of dying and soon they will fall to the ground, tossed by the breeze, they dance in the air in a final flutter of life only to come to rest in the earth, to feed the cycle of growth once more; great beauty indeed but the beauty of death, an essential part of the cycle of life. Is this why the seedling I felt grow within now appears to have withered? Is this why I weep just as before and turn away from tomorrow? Is this why I falter, lose heart and despair, consumed by the pain of his absence? Whatever it is, the progress is lost and I'll have to start out again.

Tears, Idle Tears

Tears, idle tears, I know not what they mean, tears from the depth of some divine despair rise in the heart, and gather to the eyes, in looking on the happy autumn-fields, and thinking of the days that are no more.
....
O Death in Life, the days that are no more.

Alfred Lord Tennyson 1809 – 1892

The Bird with a Broken Wing

I cannot rise from the ground, like a bird with a broken wing. Try as I might I cannot take flight, like a bird with a broken wing.

To continue to struggle is useless it only causes more pain. I must try to look for a quiet little nook to rest' til I'm better again.

Safe from predators fierce, the bird can hide in its nest but though I have tried, I cannot hide from the turmoil going on in my breast.

The bird must wait in patience 'till the feathered wing is healed then it can fly high in the sky and rejoice in the sun and the field.

But here on the ground I'm imprisoned, loss and despair hold me fast, I must learn to restrain the grief and the pain, accept that our life is now past.

Yes I too must endure with composure give time for my spirit to mend and then, if not soar, at least try once more to walk on life's way to its end.

To walk on the road with acceptance remember our life with a smile, remember the wife, but pick up my life as a widow and walk the last mile.

But oh what a hard thing to do. To walk on from all you hold dear, to hold back a tear when all you can hear is your heart crying "let me stay near".

The greatest glory of living lies not in never falling, but in rising every time you fall.

Nelson Mandela 1918 –

"Success is never permanent; failure is never fatal."
"The only thing that really counts is to never, never, never give up."

Winston Churchill 1874 – 1965

And the seedling did not die and when I felt stirrings again, in desperation I strove to keep it alive.

Then, like a ray of sunshine that breaks through the glowering clouds and sends a shaft of light across a sombre landscape, an unexpected friend, through chance circumstances realised my plight. With her complete understanding and total generosity she helped me along the stony path, found me sheltered grassy banks to rest along the way and saw me through another crisis. An embodiment of our Anglo-Spanish experiences she was a true angel in my eyes and it seems to me a miracle that out of all Cornwall we together had chosen Launceston and so there in due time I was able to find her.

No More

No more will he see the rising sun or the rainbow in the sky.
No more will he gaze o'er the fields so green wherein the cattle lie.

No more will he hear the cuckoo call or the screech of the swifts on the wing.
No more will he pause in wondrous delight to hear the skylark sing.

No more will he smell my new baked bread or the scent of his favourite coffee.
No more will he sniff at his bacon and egg or the whiff of his special toffee.

No more will he feel the heat of the sun or the bite of the winter frost.
No more will he feel the touch of my hand all this to him is now lost.

No more will he taste a birthday cake or a good old English roast.
No more will he sip a fine French wine to offer a happy toast.

No more will he sit in a Spanish bar and ask for his favourite brandy, or suggest a walk by the side of the sea, along the beach so sandy.

No more will he say "this is the life" as we enjoy something good together.
No more suggest a change of plan "to enjoy this lovely weather."

No more will he try to beat me at tennis, running me right off the court.
No more will he grin when doing a crossword and give me the answer I sought.

No more will he smile that mischievous smile as something outrageous he says.
No more will those blue eyes twinkle with glee as we walk through our joyous days.

No more will he argue, discuss and explain or tell me "this is the goods" or sit at the keyboard, playing his golf game trying to beat Tiger Woods.

No more will he go to his great pile of books, reading who-done-its or history. Then come to share what he'd found there explaining a motive or mystery.

No more will he lead and ask me to follow, so many new things to explore.
No more tell me how, or why, when and where, as he did so often before.

All that intelligence, wisdom and wit, knowledge, experience, good sense.
No more will we see it, all this he has lost, all has been taken from hence.

All that he had, all that he gave, gone from this life for ever. All lost to him and also to us, through that cruel, final sever.

No more can I greet the rising sun with hope as it smiles at me. For my love has been taken to his grave.

"And oh, the difference to me!"

My favourite poet says it so much better than I and says it all in so few words; but through those words our hearts are one and he and I through the distance and time that separate us have a complete understanding of each other, or a least I have a complete understanding of what he was feeling when he penned the beautiful poem that follows

Lucy 111

She dwelt among the untrodden ways beside the springs of Dove, A Maid whom there were none to praise and very few to love:

A violet by a mossy stone half hidden from the eye! Fair as a star, when only one is shining in the sky.

She lived unknown, and few could know When Lucy ceased to be; but she is in her grave, and oh, the difference to me!

William Wordsworth

On the Death of a Hedgehog

Next morning I got up and it did not, the first day after a death, the new absence is always the same; we should be careful of each other, we should be kind while there is still time.

Philip Larkin 1922 – 1950

It is true – the complex system that is life is all too brief. Why can't we all be kind to each other while there is still time?

Why can't we remember to "Contemplate our unity with the earth and all forms of life and existence?"

Yes, there is a huge difference to the individual between the death of a spouse and the death of a hedgehog, indeed there is a huge difference between the death of a spouse, and any other human death though all have their individual awfulness, but on another level why do we so often forget that all life is one?

This is what underlies all philosophies, all religions – goodness is love, goodness is caring and that holds for human relationships, hedgehogs, sparrows and our very planet itself.

"Are not two sparrows sold for a small coin? Yet not one of them falls to the ground without your Father's knowledge."

St Matthew

I dread the approach of the next three months as they march inexorably towards me bearing, as they do, such terrible anniversaries, such memories of grief and pain. I know that I must keep busy and then take one step at a time, focusing only on surviving for just the next moment; just the next hour, the next day; the next week until at last these months will have marched on by me and into the irretrievable past. Once more I shall need all my strength.

December

Today my ship ran aground on a submerged rock. A little thing, I had not seen it coming. I rose very early and sat in the quiet of the morning to write my Christmas cards. Of course I had to sign just my own name – the first time in nearly half a century I had done so. After an hour I could stand it no more, put down my task and returned to my bed. My faithful little black cat followed me and huddled close. There we stayed a while, two pieces of flotsam on the sea of existence until at length she began her gentle purring which eased the pain and soothed my spirit so that we were able to face the day again.

Today I went to Plymouth on the bus. I chose a raised seat at the back so that I could see over the hedges and enjoy the beautiful views all around. I had chosen an ideal day for the sky was blue and cloudless and the sun shone over the green rolling hills divided by hedgerows and stands of trees and peopled by cows, sheep and even from time to time horses standing patiently and wearing their winter blankets against the cold. It wasn't really cold but just crisp and clear, except where tendrils of early morning mist lingered in the hollows, and only the north facing slopes were lightly dusted with frost. But the beauty surrounding me so near to home pierced my heart for he could not see it and as we set out, try as I might, I couldn't prevent the tears from falling. Summoning all my strength

I composed myself and dried my eyes. The bus followed the all too familiar road but from my elevated position I saw views unseen from a car.

Then the bus made the first of its detours to pick up the country folk and took me to places we had not had the chance to find. Places like Stoke Climsland with its dear little pond, home to three white ducks. Villages of little stone cottages, white houses with slate roofs and black paintwork set alongside meandering lanes; often they were sheltered by belts of trees, some already reduced to a tracery of twigs where the rooks, appearing to stand guard beside their nests, were silhouetted against the blue sky, others like the beech still clinging to their russet autumn leaves, still more like the cotoneasters laden with red berries, a Christmas feast for the birds. In one garden I even saw a winter cherry covered in pink blossom, a true delight on a lovely crisp morning. Then the bus toiled up another hill and bowled merrily along the top of a ridge from where I could see the whole green patchwork of fields dotted with little villages often clustering round the square stone tower of a church; the so English, green beauty of the South West.

The interest of exploring new territory and the beauty of what I found soothed my spirits and I began to enjoy the journey until the bus detoured into Saltash and I was again in that main street where during our first visit to Cornwall we enjoyed lunch in a pub overlooking the beautiful bridge and made enquiries about finding a home. It was exactly two years ago, the start of an adventure and I had not been back since. Now I was here again, but alone. But on we went and as the bus crossed the road bridge I again had a better view. A train was crossing Brunel's fine bridge and I was free to gaze across the lovely river, upstream and down.

Once in town the twin experiences continued. I have obviously made some progress for this time I was able to follow my plan, see the sights and shop as we had always done together, and take in what was going on around me. I thought back to my first solo visit after his death. Despite the memories, both happy and heartbreaking, that Plymouth now held for me, I thought, in my ignorance that I could cope with it and so after returning something to the hospital I went on into the centre. But, once there I walked past and through the shops like a zombie, unseeing, uninterested, taking in nothing and I just turned and fled home. Today was different and I held my own though he was with me every step of the way, never out of my mind.

On the return journey the countryside grew more sombre as the light faded and a silvery crescent moon hung like a lamp in the still blue sky etched with the tracery of the winter bare trees. Finally it was good to be home to the welcome of the cats eager to see what treat I had brought them. Yes, a day of twin experiences but I had done it.

He cannot see

The winter landscape, still so green, although the trees are bare, and patches of frost sparkle in the sun, nature's jewels rare. I wish he could see the beauty, in this silent tranquil scene, but he is not here; and he cannot see; and he is lost to me.

The pool of bluebells in the wood is a wondrous sight to see, and the primrose springs from the grassy bank to shyly smile at me. The gambolling lambs play in the fields, the hares box on the hills, but he is not here; and he cannot see; and he is lost to me.

My full petalled roses, the essence of summer, beauty in pink and cream. Many hued borders spill out their fragrance as they sit in the sunshine and dream. The bees are all busy taking the nectar as they drone from flower to flower, but he is not here; and he cannot see; and he is lost to me.

The stooks in the meadows, the fruits in the hedgerows, the vibrant tints of the leaves. The mist of the morning, the chill of the evening when smoke curls up from the eaves, the bounty of autumn drips from each bough giving provision for winter, but he is not here; and he cannot see; and he is lost to me.

And so the year has turned its full circle as the earth spins round the sun, each season has brought its own delight as the days their courses have run, but there's no one to share its myriad sights no one to give it meaning, for he is not here; and he cannot see; and he is lost to me.

Lucy V

No motion has she now, no force; She neither hears nor sees; Roll'd round in earth's diurnal course, With rocks, and stones, and trees.

William Wordsworth

13th December

Today was one of the worst days ever. It started badly as my cold seemed much worse and I felt really ill. I stayed in bed a while but there were things to do so I got up. One of the cats wasn't well either which upset me and my phone wasn't working properly which worried me further.

I felt alone and out of my depth. I dealt with essentials and then came an unexpected visitor – the florist with a beautiful bouquet for me. It was from dear college friends reminding me that they were thinking of me at what they knew was a very difficult time with all the memories of last year to be lived through. Their thoughts and kindness reduced me to tears. Later the postman called with more sympathetic cards, among them a most beautiful work of art made by a very dear friend and sent by her and her husband also someone very special, a couple who had attended the funeral. The thought, work, care and love which had gone into this card and the message it contained completely overwhelmed me and there were more tears. In the same post was another card also beautifully and specially made for me and a third from a previous and loved neighbour, both of these written with understanding.

I suppose it was the combination of not feeling well, various problems arising during the day and the enormous love and support of friends which so overwhelmed me but in some ways my situation seemed even worse than it did last year. Perhaps the full implications of what happened take some time to be fully accepted. Then again, sometimes an act of kindness or thoughtfulness shown to a grieving person, although so very welcome, can be more upsetting than anything else. I know that I am lucky in the kindness, love and support I have been shown by friends old and new. I do not know how I could get through this without them. Today I have felt that I cannot take any more, but yet I know I must and I have to walk on. So in the end I find the strength to do as friends have suggested and after an initial resistance from my very soul, seek solace in memories of times now gone for good; and to some extent I find it.

17th December

A year ago today the horror began when the surgeon gave us the death sentence. I went to Glynn Valley. It was a beautiful day and the valley lay in the sun, calm and still under a blue sky. Such peace and beauty all around, but not within. Time has not yet started to heal but it has already given me the knowledge of what my continued existence without him really is and so the despair is deeper.

Lucy IV

She died, and left to me This heath, this calm and quiet scene; The memory of what has been, And never more will be.

William Wordsworth

Later help was at hand once more – all it takes is the courage and strength to say yes" and "thank you". Once again my kind neighbours included me – first in the children's nativity play and then in sharing a coffee and snack. As usual, it was enough to restore some calm to my aching heart.

I think of the Spanish saying

"One must learn to accept, and learn to accept …….with a smile"
Perhaps some day I will be able to do both, but today, I can do neither.

This Strange New Land

I have travelled now for about a year and I have found this strange new land. Its hills are rounded, its colours muted. Its pathways stony and hard.

This land knows no springtime nor summer nor fall. Its landscape is always the same. But its weather is fickle, can change in a second. Turn without warning to rain.

It rains a lot in this strange new land. Grey curtains of rain sweeping its hills. They soften the landscape; they deaden the air and sometimes they blot out the view.

Sometimes they're driven by violent winds stinging your face with their force. Sometimes their raindrops fall gently to earth soft as goose feather down.

At times there are storms that gather with menace overwhelming your soul with their strength. But in time they do pass and leave in their wake an exhausted sense of peace.

The landscape is quiet no crowds do I see, no laughter, no smiles and no joy. The pathways lead on; their goal is unseen but the urge to keep going is strong.

And now I meet people, gentle and kind. They pause and they smile at me. They inhabit this land, they do understand they stop and reach out a hand.

They take me with them; they show me the way. They offer me new hope of life; not life as it was, that has now gone. But life as it now must be.

They speak of their sorrows, shock and despair. They listen to my tales of woe. They nod their agreement, hold fast when I falter. Point to the corners ahead.

They show me calm byways where I can rest. Stay with me to share this repose. They show me what helps, encourage my efforts, give me oases of peace.

I see for the first time that here in our midst, It is always here this strange land but until we cross that bridge of death we really do not understand.

This land that exists right in our midst, though terrible, lonely and sad, has its own comforts, its bonds and its sharing, the sunshine that gleams through the rain.

My new friends tell me that this stony path will lead to acceptance and peace. Though the way is hard and the trek is long we do learn to smile once again.

But the death a spouse is a blow so hard that we cannot recover completely. We live with our sadness, unable to fly like a bird with a broken wing.

And this new strange new land will not go away and never more will we leave it. We will stay together and help one another in the land of the living half dead.

Yes, I find that I have a joined a sisterhood and, just as in an order of nuns, there is this bond between us and although it is death, despair and grief that has brought us together yet it is ultimately a bond of love that binds us. We understand each other's language and we share and support each other knowing there is no alternative but to journey on and make a new life. Those further down the road help the newcomers and ease their pain. Despite all, or because of all, as I travel further into this land I find there is a gentle kindness in the world of widowhood.

The intimate companionship of marriage is the best thing life has to offer.

Bertrand Russell 1872 – 1970

It's not that being a widow is dreadful – it's that being in a companionable marriage is wonderful. People die but love does not die – we carry it with us.

Mary Rogers

I know the above to be true but it takes time to appreciate that this is so, for someone who has lost their soul-mate is literally half dead as one's other half is lost and can never return. We do indeed carry that love with us into this new existence but we have to leave behind the presence and the sharing and we are literally torn apart. Having experienced "the best thing that life has to offer" it is very hard to walk on and "leave" our other half and "carrying the love with us" is both a consolation and a great pain. Only time can grant us acceptance but he does it – oh so slowly!

The end of the year

The bells ring out the end of the year. It's a sound that is welcome to me. The end of the year, the worst year of all. And there's one consolation, one comforting thought, no matter what happens, where ever I go, whatever the battles that have to be fought, nothing can ever again be so bad. I've been through the worst and survived.

January

Oh dreaded month

Oh dreaded month, now you have to be faced anew, there's no escape, whatever words are said, it's true. The past is dead, but in my heart its memories live. The memories of our life and of its dreadful end. This month visions of them both to me will send, and is it consolation or grievous pain they give as both the good and bad will haunt me through its days? And though I try to deal with them in many ways they have their gruesome hour and will not be denied. As yet, the sev'rance is too new and pain they bring but though they hurt so much I cannot help but cling. When one half dies the other loses life; yet lives, and in this state, unable to forget, accept, however strong the will to fight my eyes have wept. So Time where is thy mercy? I can only turn to thee.

14th January

Today marks a year, a year that I have been without him; the pain and grief are no less but the knowledge of what his absence means is greater and so the path I tread still leads downwards.

Glynn Valley beautiful as ever lay quietly, as did my saddened spirit. Later, after a pleasant meal with the friend who accompanied me, I fled home alone and in tears.

Time where is thy silken mist?

Time where is thy silken mist? When will you lay it over my world. Let its gentleness soothe my spirit. Its mellow folds ease my heart with its merciful misty blur?

I grow so weary under this burden. His absence so hard to carry along. Its weight so heavy, its size so great that it blots out the light of the living sun and leaves me forlorn in this valley of shades.

Time you are my only hope. When will you tame the rage of my grief, raise my gaze to a new existence, lift my hand to life and friend and soften the stones beneath my feet?

I know only you can bring some acceptance. Teach resignation to all HE has lost. Lull my senses and dim the pain. Allay my suffering, temper my hurt and reconcile me to what now must be.

But how much longer must I struggle. What pangs of despair must I feel. How keenly feel the loss of he who meant the world and more to me. Before you take pity and yield to my plea?

For one long year I've walked this path leading only down and down ever deeper, ever sharper into the vale of death and loss into the knowledge of what is left.

Truly many friends support me but only you can blunt this pain. Why so slow to show compassion, lay your gentle touch on me and soothe my aching heart.

I know this burden is for always. It's not my wish to ever forget. Nothing can replace what has been lost; but your merciful mists can blur my distress and help me to face the days I have left.

Once again I have found someone reaching out over distance and time and expressing far more eloquently than I the emotions I now feel so keenly. I can match his emotions but he soars far above me in leaving for us the truly beautiful poem that follows.

Time and Grief

O Time! Who know'st a lenient hand to lay softest in sorrow's wound, and slowly thence (Lulling to sad repose the weary sense) The faint pang stealest unperceived away; On thee I rest my only hope at last, And think, when thou hast dried the bitter tear That flows in vain o'er all my soul held dear, I may look back on every sorrow past, And meet life's peaceful evening with a smile: As some lone bird, at days departing hour, Sings in the sunbeam, of the transient shower forgetful, though its wings are wet the while:- Yet ah! How much must this poor heart endure, Which hopes from thee, and thee alone, a cure!

William Lisle Bowles 1762 – 1850

She walks in twilight

She walks in twilight surrounded by the mists of time, the washed out colours of her world tinged grey with sadness. She lifts her eyes to leaden lowering skies their clouds reflected in the watery landscapes of her world. Here no flowers can grow, no birds can sing; here all is stilled, barren, dark and empty, disturbed only by the moaning of the wind and the pattering of the rain. Why does she walk in such a sterile land? Resolute, she trudges on, she has no choice. There is no rest, no joy, no sun. For the light of her life is gone.

Death Thou Art Most Cruel

Death thou art most cruel, thy touch will steal the whole away. Thy cold hand snuffs the flame of life and takes from one his all. Where once was love and laughter, joy and hope for the coming day. Remains a cold insensate shell made lifeless by thy call.

Though not his humour, nor his courage, responded to your voice, you sapped the strength and dimmed the mind, once so quick and agile. Independence too you stole, and dignity and choice reducing fierce determination, to impotence so fragile.

But even this is not enough thy cruelty to assuage, All from one, is just the start, for what do you leave behind? Through one, you touch so many more who with that life engage they too are robbed, but you heed not, unto their grief so blind.

And if there is a special one you snatch at that life too, Break its heart, crush its spirit, eager to make your mark. Leave it blind to try to stand and make a life anew. Struggling to come from under your shadow, trying to climb out of the dark.

More dead than alive you leave it; you have no mercy, no remorse in handing down your burden of empty loss and piteous pain. You make its broken spirit continue on, in its lonely course. Fearing, despite its efforts, it can never really touch life again.

Yes, in the one and in them all, the difference thou hast made spreads ever wider from thy touch like ripples on a pond. But we will prevail, for in our hearts memories never fade. And in those hearts we carry the one, of whom we are so fond.

This love is stronger than thy work and so we have him still. You've taken his presence but cannot touch his life so deep within. It's not the same we must admit but we'll go on, 'til the day you come to claim us too, the day you finally win.

He whom we love and lose is no longer where he was before. He is now wherever we are.

**St John Chrysostom –
Bishop living in C4th AD**

A year ago today there was a funeral – and close by, another death – two women newly widowed became friends, each understanding the other's pain. Today we shared a simple meal and the friends who supported us brought vintage port and proposed a toast to the two we had lost. Thus we survived another day.

You

You were the sparkle in my seconds, the companionable murmuring stream in my minutes, the constant joy of my waking hours. You were the beauteous mystery of my early dawns, the golden sunshine of all my days, the radiant splendour of my evening sunsets and the shining moonbeams of my nights.

You were the deepest meaning of my weeks. The soul mate of my years. You were the snowdrops in my winters Heralding the renewing strength of life. You were the burgeoning green of my spring times bringing bloom to all you touched.

You were the peace and ease of all my summers, your love like the warmth of the sun above. You were the abundant harvests of my autumns, resplendent richness you have brought, the soul mate of my years.

You were the companion of my decades staying ever close by my side, for more than half a century always there, a loving guide. Love and laughter you brought to me as through the years we two have travelled. Now you are gone and I'm left alone. Alone and lost without my treasure, the soul mate of my years.

February

Today marks a year that all that is left of him has lain on that hill overlooking the peaceful scene. Another visit to Glynn Valley was planned but Nature intervened. Thick snow overnight made travel impossible. I bowed to circumstance and spent the day quietly with my memories. The last of the first anniversaries is now behind me. I take down the beautiful card made and sent by my friends, which has been there during the past cruel weeks and read again, as so many times before, its lovely message of support. Then it is laid carefully away. Once more I have survived but now I must go on.

More than a year has passed

More than a year has passed. I've made some changes, gained new friends, Found new things to do. I've built a new life but that's not enough I have to live it too.

So now it has to be faced, the hardest thing I've ever done, the worst act of them all, I have to walk into that life, drink the cup of gall.

Time is growing impatient; but I cling to him and can't let go. He's every waking thought. His burly presence ever in my mind, just as love has taught.

Its not that I must forget but more that I have to learn to remember; Acknowledge the distance of death, carry him with me and love him still, remember with every breath.

But I'm going on alone. He cannot share in the new life I've made, the life I am forced to tread. I must let go the substance, acknowledge the ghost and learn to live with the dead.

I like my little house with its clean modern lines. It is filled with my favourite colours and favourite things. Memories of our life together, pieces we chose together, his rugs, pictures and photographs, our books and music, my embroideries and other things I made. English things and Spanish things, others from our travels and still more that were gifts from friends. Each one brings a memory of people and places; each one can bring a smile to my lips. It's quiet and peaceful here and the tiny enclosed garden is safe for the cats. Yes, it is an oasis, a safe haven and when I come home the cats come running to the door to greet me. It's a friendly cosy place.

Last night, after a peaceful day, I looked around at the things that pleased me and suddenly, without warning, I shouted out – "its waiting for you; the house is waiting for you". The thought was so strong it overwhelmed me for I know that it waits in vain.

Today, on an errand I drove through some very pretty, quiet little villages, I saw a small wood completely carpeted with snowdrops and several of the country lanes had patches of them on their banks and in their hedgerows. What a beautiful county Cornwall is at all seasons. Its beauty overwhelmed me because I cannot share it. How he would have loved today but all this he has lost.

March

At last the three "dreaded months" have passed by me and "marched on into the irretrievable past". I was right to fear them and have indeed again needed all my strength to survive, as they brought me not only what I had feared but more.

There was no easing, no softening, only reliving of the unbelievable, a new emphasis on all HE had lost and a greater realisation of what it meant for me. The path still leads downwards.

Indeed there was more, for also during this time I lost first, and to an unexpected and instantaneous death, a good friend who had been very kind to me and days later, having called the vet to attend one of my beloved cats, had to face the advice "the time has come", and so I had to take her and hold her while she was humanely put to sleep. Although I knew it was the right thing to do, I felt a murderess and mourn her still.

So these were dark days indeed and although, as always, I was determined to overcome all this, there were times when there was a new fear – I feared I could fail.

The door has closed

Yes, the door has closed. Maybe with this too there will be false starts and relapses, as has happened so often before that I am unpredictable even to myself, but nevertheless there has been a change. It is as if, although my head has known the truth, my wayward heart could not let go and kept one desperate foot in the door to keep it open just a little. So although I had built a new life I wasn't really in it. I wasn't really living it but just going through the motions. Perhaps during these last terrible three months I realised the danger this ever deepening despair now presented and the genuine fear of failure pulled me up. Perhaps my friends, old and new, have succeeded in really reaching me and pulling me on and new interests have engaged with me at last.

Whatever the explanation, for over a week now I have felt this change. I am here and he is there and I am living my life rather than clinging to ours. Oh, the pain is still there and I have still wept but there is an acceptance and, even more, a connection to present reality that was not there before.

Although carrying him with me I am living my own agenda. The door has closed and, though in sorrow, I have moved away from it. Perhaps the path is turning upwards?

Today was one of those days when everything I touched seemed to go wrong – lots of small problems and especially with the computer which always get to me. Eventually there were tears and I told myself I was behaving like a spoilt child but oh,

I miss him so and not least when things go wrong. How much I miss him when things go wrong!

This morning I woke and remembered yesterday – so I reminded myself that "being positive is a choice". I will see to it that today will be another busy day.

This evening I went to the computer club. It was a most interesting and entertaining session based on photographs and video – magnificent scenery, wonderful animal shots, humour and unbelievable occurrences. I really enjoyed it and left the meeting happy. As I walked out into the street I thought how much he would have enjoyed it too. Within seconds I was in tears and once home there were more.

How much he has been denied. How much I miss him when things go right!

Benevolent presence

I have always felt that he was and always will be a part of my life even though his physical presence is lost to me and indeed expressed this in one of the verses of the poem I wrote for his interment.

But though I feel lonely I'm not really alone, You live in my memory and heart so forlorn. There you will stay and be with me still in good times and bad, just as before.

But until now, as with so many other things, there has been almost a disconnection, certainly an overwhelming feeling that this is not enough. But today a doctor when talking to me used the phrase "a benevolent presence" – "a benevolent presence in your life" and somehow I connected to this, my mind coalesced round this thought and I accepted it. I have to live my own agenda but he is a part of my life not just in memory, or in the emptiness left by his loss, but in his ongoing influence. I remember his ways, his attitudes to things and his advice, of course I do.

All of this is now truly a part of me; more than fifty years of sharing have inevitably influenced my growth and development just as I influenced his. Truly that still lives and is part of what I am. I see now that he is truly with me in more ways than I have realised. It is not just that I carry him with me but he is still part of me. Our marriage is over as death has parted us but it cannot destroy the one entity that we became during that marriage. The line from the poem I quoted above which now adorns his memorial plaque and which I repeat here

"If ever two were one than surely we"

Is still as true as it was when we both lived. It is not just that I carry him with me in memory, he is with me, he is part of me still. No it is not enough and it never will be, but it is more than I realised and it is something. He is still indeed, in so many ways, "a benevolent presence" in my life.

I remember the words of the 4th Century Bishop I quoted above. I have rebelled against those words, crying that they are a mere shadow and empty consolation, but now I see the wisdom they contain, a wisdom coming down to me from over 2000 years ago.

He whom we love and lose is no longer where he was before. He is now wherever we are.

**St John Chrysostom –
Bishop living in C4th AD**

And so as I go on with my new life I can truly say

You,
and our love,
live still,
in my heart.

May

I have thought a great about deal this "benevolent presence" and what it means.

I know I have been lucky to have shared so much of my life with him and I always knew it would not go on for ever, that sooner or later death would come and one of us would have to walk on alone. Time has shown that I am that one and now I return to the words from his service –

"enjoy your memories of him just as you have today, resolving that you who live on, will use your lives more fully and to better purpose for having known him or for having shared in his life"

I, above all others, must heed those words. This is what I must do now, indeed it is the only thing left that I can do for him – live my life more fully and to better purpose – so that in some small way the world continues to be a better place because he has lived in it. So many have reached out to me and supported me, so much still remains to be done. I must give back to friends old and new; I must live with purpose so that WE continue to live and his "benevolent presence" is felt to the full. To do anything less would be let him down. I must not let grief maim the rest of life or bring darkness to those who offer to me their friendship, love and support. Grieve for him I always will but it must be in the context of happy memories and positive living. This is why I must

"smile at the life-giving sun"

July

And so once again I reached out to Peace.

And finally She came.

And Peace Came

And eventually Peace came in the silence of dawn. Her footsteps so light they harmed not the dew, her movements so gentle I saw not her approach.

Enfolding me in her arms she hushed my fever, she soothed my spirit and calmed my soul, she held me in her stillness and breathed her tranquillity.

Gently she spoke to me of all we had had, all we had been, all we had done, all we had shared, though now all was gone.

On she went – it's no longer the present but its still your past and that lives on supporting your days and consoling your nights.

What you had was a precious jewel. A shining crystalline globe of love; a glowing bubble lighter than air.

It floated through time a beauteous thing. Ephemeral as a rainbow with its colours of light, as fragile as a flower in the vast winds of time.

Do not cry for the ways things are. Be happy you were given the gift of life. Be happy that you enjoyed the wonder that is love.

Do not mourn the progress of time. The beauty of the rainbow is no less because it fades, the charm of a smile no less because it's brief.

What you have left, still must be grasped and lived to the full, it's what he would want. Even now, what you have is a beauteous thing.

Don't turn your back on the miracle of life. Embrace each new day with its trials and gifts, its friendships, its beauties, its hardships and storms.

I knew in my heart the wisdom of her words. They gave me the calm and the strength to go on. And I responded to the truth they contained.

But I still had a question and turned to her once more Peace, you can't help me with all He has lost, and that I will mourn for the rest of my days.

No my dear child, that too you must accept. That too is part of the progress of time He too had his hour and be thankful for that.

He too had his place in the bubble of light. Had his shining crystalline globe of love. He too has been blessed and he knew it.

In the stillness of night she stole quietly away leaving her gifts of harmony and peace leaving me the strength to face a new dawn.

She left too the knowledge, that life must go on and we must accept the way that things are and take our place in all that occurs.

Constantly changing, life rushes on weaving its threads of such varied existence and some of these threads are cruel and dark.

But despite all that we must embrace each hour, face it with calm and play our best part for the fabric life weaves is a marvellous thing.

I know that I will always carry the burden of this loss, I know that there will be days when I move forward and others when my steps are backwards; days of calm and acceptance, even enjoyment, and some when even a single thought will plunge me back down; but at least I know that life must go on and I must go on with it, and look back with gratitude for all that I had and forward with appreciation of what I have now.

The Old Oak Tree

Though old and gnarled, it stands so firm, its branches reaching for the blue sky beyond, its leaves so green, its flowers though small responding with life to the warmth of the sun.

It casts its shade o'er the flowers at its feet and the creatures of the forest, that come to rest there. It offers a haven to those who can climb and shelter to the birds as they build their new nests.

It's home to myriads of tiny things that creep or crawl, jump, fly or hop, some so tiny they're hard to see others so hidden they're easy to miss.

Some are bigger and catch our attention, as beating their wings or waving their feelers they fly and dive or amble along the way of life mapped out for them.

A tree is a world in itself you see. Full of life, movement and song but look at this one a little more closely something's amiss, something is wrong.

That branch there, devoid of leaf, this one here, where the leaf is sere; look more closely, see that wound the tree is hollow and slowly dying.

Great oak tree so old and gnarled, you stand so firm and reach for the sky. Like me you seem strong and responsive to life but part of your life is ended and gone.

I look at the tree and see my own self, that busy exterior engagement with life but under the surface something has died and just like the tree I'm hollow inside.

My new life swirls round me, busy and full, sometimes it's pleasant sometimes it's peaceful, new goals give it purpose, good friends give it warmth, but that inner hollow just won't go away.

September

Today I went once more to Glynn Valley. Just before I left, in a chance encounter someone said to me

"How are you? How are you doing?"

My usual response to this question rose my lips

"Oh not so bad thank you."

But this was the man who had led the funeral service, a man who had been very kind to me and I thought to myself – he deserves, a better answer than that stock, polite deflection – and so choking back tears, I added

> "the veneer is a little stronger but everything else is just the same".

He said to me

"Sometimes you hear something and it sticks with you; one thing that has always stuck with me since I first heard it is this –

> "Grief is the price we pay for love"

I smiled and we agreed – that says it all doesn't it.

I left still smiling, my spirits lifted, for after all it is true and when looked at in that way, though it is higher than I could possibly have imagined, I have to acknowledge it is a price worth paying.

Yes

> It is a price worth paying.

October

A dear friend takes me on a magical trip to St Michael's Mount.

I truly enjoyed her kindness and thoughtfulness; the exotic gardens displaying their treasures in the autumn sunshine; the sea and sky all around, above and below, reflecting the spinning beauty of the glowing blue planet we call Earth; the grey fortress towering above, its guns pointing outwards to sea and shore; the simple stone church, calm yet almost forbidding, its plain altar adorned with rich golden embroidery. Outside there is such beauty – a gift of existence. Inside an ancient reminder of the business of man – his works and his strivings; his quarrels and fights, his search for peace and meaning.

I think back to the first visit she planned for me, shortly after his death. That time we went to Caerhays Castle to walk in the woods and enjoy the wonderful magnolias, azaleas and rhododendrons. That too was a day of beauty and should have been a day of pleasure, just as she had planned, but although I went through the motions all was dust in my mouth; my face smiled while my heart wept; my feet walked on while I lay on the ground and although she is such a good friend I felt forced to be dishonest and not let her see the pain in every second. He would have loved this but he is not here, he is not here.

Today was truly different. Something is stronger.

We have a new member in our Spanish group. She has joined for the same reason I did – having lived in Spain and studied the language she does not want to lose it now that she is back in England. I welcomed her entry into my life, I was pleased and happy – another piece in the jigsaw of the new life I am building, I thought. But that thought was treacherous, a false friend, for it brought another in its wake – yes, another step onwards – and also another step away from him, something else he knows nothing about! My peace destroyed, I banged and screamed at the bars of my prison. How do I free myself from this cage that holds me? Every little success, every fight to move on, every time I reach out to life, although I do it and know that I must, it always flips over to the reverse of the coin – I'm moving away without him. And so once more, each new strength is also a new pain.

Once again a good friend was there to help me with his words of wisdom and spoke to me of the true difference between moving on and moving away. How lucky I have been in friends!

Later I thought of my friend's words wanting to reject them.

"They are just words".
"The way he is with me now is just words".
"No it's more than that but it's a pale shadow,
　　　　A Will o'the wisp, a ghost".

"No that's not true; he is part of you still".

The battle raged on, my head acknowledging the sense spoken by my friend but my heart and soul screaming no! Oh, the desperation of bereavement! At last some acknowledgement came and I gained the strength to accept the positive and cope with the negative. I continued onwards.

November

Suddenly, I realise with surprise that, although we are already halfway through November and Christmas will soon be upon us, this time I had not seen the approach of the three months I had so rightly dreaded last year; and now that I do notice them I see that they have lost their terrible power. I am too busy to listen to their screams. This time round it is they who are in the bubble while I am in the real world. Yes, December and January will still bring their awful memories but that is all they are – memories. I hope that this new strength will last. Perhaps that battle in the cage will prove to be a turning point. I smile and taking his hand in mine I walk with him into the future.

December

Weeks later this new strength is still with me. Perhaps the trap is really sprung and I am out of the cage. I hope so but whatever is in store I know that every time I fall, if fall I must, his "benevolent presence" will help me to rise and move on.

I walk with him into the future.

March

A Homecoming

Once more I wing my way to Spain, as a migratory bird returns to its nest.

Yes, I am making another visit but this time there is a difference. This time I am going back to that little piece of Spain that was ours. Good friends who had visited us there many times rang to tell me they had rented an apartment for two months. "I will come and visit you" I said without thinking.

I came off the phone and then stood appalled. "What I have done?" I asked myself. "How can I go back without him?" For a while I was horrified – "I can't do this. What was I thinking of?" After a while I calmed down "this is silly, of course you can do it he wouldn't want you to stay away". And so, although later I confessed my doubts to my friends I overcame them and determined to go.

Three months passed and the appointed time arrived. I set off with no idea of how I was going to react despite the "Yes, this is the right thing to do. Of course I will be alright". There were other friends to visit too, all the Spanish friends I had made. So I boarded the plane. I had become used to flying alone, almost enjoyed it, but this time would be different; a return to where paradise had existed. As usual at take off, he felt very close to me for whenever we had flown, at this moment he always reached for my hand and held it until we were aloft and on our way. Now the revving of the engines at the end of the runway always brings him near.

It was a good flight. We soared towards the sun and I looked down once more to that green patchwork that is south-west England; then the sea, this time so blue, and on through wispy cloud catching glimpses of the west coast of France as we steadily flew south. Lunch diverted my attention and then suddenly a glance outside made me catch my breath. We were over the high Pyrenees and below stretched a magical world of gleaming peaks, glistening in the sun; one after another so pure and white guarding mottled hidden valleys in their curves and folds. "Oh, look at that" I said to the stranger next to me, for truly it was a sight not to be missed. Further and further south we flew but were above cloud as we neared Alicante. I looked at their ever changing contours, so real and yet so unsubstantial – unknown and unfathomable just like the world I was fast approaching. What would it be? What would I feel? We began our descent and I waited and watched. Suddenly we broke through the cloud and there it was - the familiar, dun, mountainous terrain I knew so well. "I'm coming home" I thought. And although Cornwall is now my home and Cornwall is where I stay, I knew the thought to be true.

Unerringly this tiny bird a fragile being struggling on, faces the elements, braves
The winds and driven on by force unknown it seeks its home, a place to rest.

It was an unexpected and propitious start. Soon we had landed and there were my friends, not just to welcome me but, as I soon discovered, to envelop me in such care and consideration that, without knowing it, they carried me forward and rooted me in the present. It was as if I had been in a hot air balloon, floating high in a world of my own and now I came to rest on the solid ground.

I didn't have to pretend; I didn't have to hide grief or despair; I didn't have to feign interest in something that in reality was dust in my mouth.

I looked at the town and saw only happy memories. I looked at the little hill nestling for protection into the southern lee of the higher mountains behind and saw only beautiful, happy memories. Both had moved on while I had been away, the little hill so much so that it didn't even look like our little hill anymore.

For the very first time I really knew that I had indeed moved on and I had indeed, truly, not moved away. The trap was sprung.

We visited places old and new, known and unknown. We walked and talked and remembered him often. They gave me something Cornwall can't give me, for except when I see the one dear friend who knew him, no one there has any memory of him. Here our memories entwined. A comment from them would set us off, or sometimes a recollection of mine would stir something in them. Familiar places were just the same, and yet no, they were different. They had moved on, the world has moved on and, yes, I have moved on but not away, he is still at my side, in my mind and my heart, wherever I am...Just as the Bishop said so long ago.

> My path leads on and I must follow, face the challenge, pass the test
> there's so much to do to pay my dues for in my life I've had the best.

Closure

And so, coming to the end of this tribute to my husband, I am reminded of the words of an old Mexican poem.

Very close to my sunset, I bless you, life……………..

Its true my vigour will be followed by winter: but you never led me to believe that May would be eternal! Without doubt I encountered long nights of sorrow; but you never promised me only good nights; and then again – I had some of heavenly calm………………..

I have loved, I was loved. The sun caressed my face.

Life you don't owe me anything. Life we are at peace.

Amado Nervo 1870 – 1919

"Every time I fall, if fall I must, his "benevolent presence" will help me to rise and move on

I walk with him into the future"

Lightning Source UK Ltd.
Milton Keynes UK
UKHW010919270620
365672UK00005B/1367